D0422173

Presented to:

—————————————

From:

—————————————

Date:

—————————————

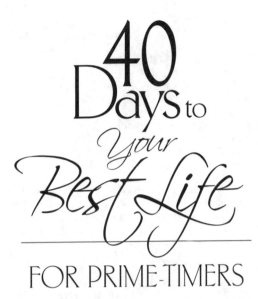

40 Days to Your Best Life

FOR PRIME-TIMERS

Overcoming the Challenges
of Senior Living

JOE RAGONT · JIM DYET

HONOR HB BOOKS

Inspiration and Motivation for the Seasons of Life

COOK COMMUNICATIONS MINISTRIES
Colorado Springs, Colorado · Paris, Ontario
KINGSWAY COMMUNICATIONS, LTD.
Eastbourne, England

Honor® is an imprint of
Cook Communications Ministries, Colorado Springs, CO 80918
Cook Communications, Paris, Ontario
Kingsway Communications, Eastbourne, England

40 DAYS TO YOUR BEST LIFE FOR PRIME-TIMERS
© 2006 by Joe Ragont and Jim Dyet

The Web addresses (URLs) recommended throughout this book are
solely offered as a resource to the reader. The citation of these Web
sites does not in any way imply an endorsement on the part of the
author or the publisher, nor does the author or publisher vouch for
their content for the life of this book.

Cover Design: BMB Design
Cover Photo Credit: © Getty Images
Interior design by Sandy Flewelling/TrueBlue Design
Interior photo © Andreas Vitting

First Printing, 2006
Printed in the United States of America

2 3 4 5 6 7 8 9 10 Printing/Year 10 09 08 07 06

Unless otherwise noted, Scripture quotations are taken from the *Holy Bible,
New International Version®*. NIV®. Copyright © 1973, 1978, 1984 by
International Bible Society. Used by permission of Zondervan. All rights
reserved. Quotations marked NKJV are taken from the New King James
Version. Copyright © 1982 by Thomas Nelson, Inc. Used by permission. All
rights reserved; quotations marked KJV are taken from the King James
Version of the Bible. (Public Domain); and quotations marked NASB are
taken from the *New American Standard Bible,* Copyright © 1960, 1995 by
The Lockman Foundation. Used by permission.

ISBN-13: 978-1-56292-383-9
ISBN-10: 1-56292-383-8

To my favorite senior, my wife.
I love you, Pat.
—Joe

To the many seniors
who have called me
"Pastor" and encouraged me
in my walk with the Lord.
—Jim

CONTENTS

Section 5: Activeness

Section 6: Death

Section 7: Planned Living

Foreword

JOE RAGONT AND JIM DYET are two of the youngest seniors I know—and I know a few. (In fact, I recently hit the speed-limit birthday myself, fifty-five, so I'm hard on their heels.) They're funny guys, which keeps them young. We occasionally golf together, and that requires every bit of their humor. (Jim is the only one of us with a clue on the course.)

While they know how to laugh and have a good time—a great tonic at any age—they also keep their priorities straight and know how and when to be serious. Though they're past conventional retirement age, neither has checked out of the world of vibrant living and ministering. Everybody knows you don't have to be in full-time Christian work to be a full-time Christian.

Spend enough time with Jim and Joe in this book and you'll be entertained, informed, humored, and inspired. Best of all, their care for people and nurture of spiritual lives comes through on every page. Though it's unlikely you've met either of them, you'll feel brought under their wings of care just as if you had.

You're in for a treat. Read this book through in one sitting or dip into it for a bite of refreshment over forty days. The result will be the same. You'll be different when you're through.

Jerry B. Jenkins

Introduction

I COULDN'T wait to get out of there.

My mother and I had driven my grandmother to the home where she would spend the rest of her life. It wasn't bad—bright and mostly clean. The staff seemed pleasant and helpful. And it was the best place we could find for the money.

Grandma certainly wasn't complaining. At ninety-two she hadn't spoken for years.

Worse, she had become incontinent. For nine years my mother had lovingly attended to her every need. But now the care Grandma required demanded strength and energy far beyond my mother's capacity.

Grandma was assigned a bed, and I sensed her involuntary compliance. Before we left, I told her how much I loved her. Her eyes blinked wide open for the first time in months, as if to say, "You're not leaving me, are you?"

There wasn't much choice.

As my mother and I left, Esther, one of the residents in her eighties, grabbed my sleeve and sobbed, "Please, mister, please help me. Take me with you. Please do something for me. Just talk to me."

I broke free and tried to say something comforting as I gathered up my mother and made for the door. I glanced back at the little lady with the hopeless expression on her tear-stained face.

Days passed, but I couldn't get that image out of my head. I felt frustrated, angry, and guilty. Two weeks later my grandmother died, as did all ties with that facility.

It has been more than fifteen years, and I still think often of Esther. Maybe more so now that I've passed that magic age of sixty-five. I wonder about all the Esthers of this world and how they deal with the devastation and loneliness that aging can bring.

I searched for resources that speak to these unique problems, but I came up empty.

I know lasting peace comes only from the Lord Jesus Christ, the Prince of Peace. As I thought about this truth, I felt the Lord leading me to develop practical help based in the Scriptures in the form of short devotional pieces that would comfort and encourage seniors. Beginning each devotional with a Scripture verse, I wanted to present relevant situations from life with corresponding examples from the Bible to leave the reader with a feeling of hope and comfort in the situations the elderly typically experience.

It was at this point that the Lord brought two longtime friends into the project.

Jerry Jenkins, best-selling author of more than 150 books and coauthor of the immensely popular *Left Behind* series, took time to encourage me and even serve as a behind-the-scenes editor on many of my contributions. Jerry has been a close friend for almost thirty years, and I was thrilled when he agreed to write the foreword.

The second was Jim Dyet, who graciously offered to write some of the devotionals for the book. Jim has written a number of devotional books for a variety of audiences, all based solidly in the Scriptures. His many years as a pastor, as well as a writer of Christian material, has given him the kind of practical experience this sort of book needed.

I'm so grateful for the involvement of each of these brothers in Christ, and I know they share my hope that this book will provide hope and comfort for those who are facing discouragement and despair.

For the glory of God,
Joe Ragont

Section 1 · LONELINESS

Day 1: A Volunteer for Jesus

Never be lacking in zeal,
but keep your spiritual fervor, serving the Lord.
—Romans 12:11

VOLUNTEERISM MAY not run a nation, but can any nation run smoothly and efficiently without it? Probably not. Volunteers are the foot soldiers who carry meals to the homebound. They are the friends who draw alongside the lonely and offer them companionship and encouragement. They are the drivers who transport the infirm to doctors' offices. They are the helpers who carry sunshine to hospital patients. They are the mentors who give students a better under-standing of math and English. They are the coaches who train kids to hit a baseball or shoot hoops. They are the men and women who drop off clothing and personal items at missions. And they are the church work-ers who perform a thousand tasks that make it a little easier for others to worship and fellowship.

Approximately 109 million American adults—56 percent of all adults—volunteer annually, contributing an average of 3.5 hours per week for a total of 20 billion hours. That's a positive commentary on what Shakespeare called "the milk of human kindness."

No one knows how many of our fellow citizens are lonely, but the number must reach into the millions. Many of them reside in nursing homes, where they hope a family member or friend will visit them. But often their hope goes unfulfilled. So they feel lonely, even abandoned. However, a visit by a friendly, caring volunteer could dispel that.

LORD, *give me your love for those who are alone or abandoned. Give me opportunities and ideas of how I might become a volunteer for you.*

Day 2: Feeling Rejected?

He was despised and rejected by men,
a man of sorrows, and familiar with suffering.
—Isaiah 53:3

COULD ANYTHING be worse than being the last kid chosen for baseball? You remember, don't you, how that works? Two of the oldest kids in a group take turns selecting their respective teams' players. Usually the kid judged to be the best player is chosen first, then the pickings get slimmer and slimmer until only one kid is left standing alone.

Unfortunately, feelings of rejection can stab us later in life too. We ask a girl for a date, but she turns us down. We submit an application for a job, but Human Resources never gets back to us. We wait for a bus, but the driver tells us he doesn't have room for us. "Another bus will be along in ten minutes," he says. We attend a social function where we are the only senior citizen, and we get ignored more often than the zucchini and horseradish dip.

Rejection can leave us feeling lonely, unwanted, and deeply hurt, but we can overcome those emotional injuries. We can remind ourselves that we made it to our senior years; others didn't. We can recall our successes along the way: We were productive employees, loving parents, good citizens, and devoted worshippers of God. We can assure ourselves that we still have a lot to contribute: experience, knowledge, wisdom, and skills. And we can count on the fact that God accepts us just as we are.

Jesus understands what it means to be rejected. More than two millennia ago, he came into the world he had created. He came bringing love and the gift of eternal life. But even his own countrymen rejected him, and the nation's religious leaders called for his execution. Worse yet, his disciples and most of his family members forsook him when he needed them most. Alone, despised, and rejected by man—and God—he suffered on the cross for you and me.

By his death Jesus opened heaven's door for each of us, and he opens his arms today to embrace us when we need a friend.

LORD, *knowing that you were rejected so that your Father could accept me unconditionally as a member of his family, I feel loved. Help me to love you better and to share your love with others.*

Day 3: Is Anyone Listening?

He who has ears to hear, let him hear!
—Matthew 11:15 NKJV

REMEMBER BEFORE television, when families gathered around the radio? We laughed at funnymen like Jack Benny, Red Skelton, and Bob Hope. We solved mysteries with Ellery Queen, Sam Spade, and Boston Blackie. We were captivated by dramas like *Suspense, Inner Sanctum*, and *Lux Radio Theatre*. And mother couldn't clean the house or prepare dinner without the companionship of Ma Perkins or Stella Dallas.

Radio was great because we could use our imaginations and picture our favorite characters any way we liked. As we listened, we provided the various images as the stories unfolded.

Youngsters who grew up in the thirties and forties learned by listening. Each day teachers in elementary school would read stories to their students who would listen intently and devour every word. Again and again, each child's active imagination would create the scenery, costumes, and props, as well as the characters' appearance for each exciting story.

Listening will always be an imperative part of our lives. But how often do people today take the time to listen to those around them? They sometimes get the self-centered idea that what they have to say is so much more important than what others are saying to them.

Many seniors complain that no one ever listens to their opinions, especially no one in the younger generation. We feel what we have to contribute isn't appreciated or under-stood, so why bother to state our opinion? It may be important and need to be heard, but how do we get others to listen?

Maybe the answer is that we need to listen first. If we do, there's a good chance we'll build relationships and trust so when it's our turn to talk, others will be apt to listen to us.

When the Lord Jesus wanted to empha-size or call attention to something he had said, he often exclaimed, "He who has ears, let him hear!"

The next time we get the insatiable urge to take control of a conversation, let's pause for a moment and listen. We just might hear some-thing that God has prepared especially for us.

LORD, *make me sensitive to what others have to say, and give me words that will honor you and help them.*

Day 4: Lonely in the Lone Star State

So do not fear, for I am with you;
do not be dismayed, for I am your God.
—Isaiah 41:10

MARSHA HAS LIVED in a small town in West Texas all her life. But at eighty she is overwhelmed with feelings of loneliness and despair. Six years ago her husband, Tad, died, leaving her with memories built over fifty-seven years of marriage. Together they had raised two daughters, both of whom married, had children, and moved to northeastern states about fifteen years before Tad passed away. They came home for their father's funeral, but Marsha hasn't seen them since then. Poor health keeps her close to home, and her daughters tell her their lives are so hectic they can't find any time for a trip to Texas.

Marsha's neighbors and friends from church stop by occasionally to check on her, but Marsha says they can't fill the void created by the loss of her husband and the distance between her and her daughters and grandchildren. Recently, she confided to her pastor's wife, "I wish the Lord would take me to heaven instead of letting me endure such loneliness. I lie awake at night and cry because I miss my family so much."

Loneliness isn't always caused by aloneness. It's possible to be surrounded by a crowd and still feel lonely. Loneliness is the heart crying out for loving relationships. Thousands of seniors experience loneliness because they are separated from a spouse by death and their children and grandchildren by distance.

Lonely people may never regain full emotional well-being, but they can help get their minds off their plights and learn how to cope with their negative feelings. Here are a few suggestions:

- Request that family members give prepaid phone cards as birthday and Christmas gifts. Talking to loved ones by phone can't take the place of a face-to-face visit, but it cheers the heart nonetheless.

- Invest in a computer and learn how to send and receive e-mail messages. Thousands of men and women in their eighties have recently joined the online millions, enjoying almost instant communication with family and friends. One newcomer to the Internet joined an online crochet club and receives as many as three hundred e-mail messages a day. Last Valentine's Day, she received valentines from online buddies throughout the nation.

- Become a pet owner. A dog or a cat can be a wonderful companion, and some tropical fish owners swear their guppies smile at them.
- Force yourself to get out more often. Meet the girls or the guys for lunch occasionally or for a cheap cup of coffee and pancakes at the Golden Arches.
- Last, but not least, acknowledge the Lord's presence. Memorize Bible promises, and talk to the Lord throughout the day.

Life isn't exactly a bowl of cherries. Sometimes it's more like a bowl of unripe persimmons. It was often like that to the first-century Hebrew Christians. The Romans hated them, and their countrymen despised them. Hounded and harassed, those early Christians got discouraged occasionally, and they must have felt lonely at times. But the writer of the letter to the Hebrews gave them a pep talk. He urged them to run the race of faith with perseverance. "Let us fix our eyes on Jesus," he advised, noting that Jesus had endured suffering and even crucifixion (see Heb. 12:1–3). Then, before closing his letter, he echoed God's promise, "Never will I leave you; never will I forsake you" (13:5).

Tasting loneliness may be like eating unripe persimmons, but staying close to Jesus is like pouring a generous helping of sugar into the bowl.

LORD, I'M LONELY. *I miss my spouse and my family. Help me conquer this vicious enemy, loneliness, in your strength. Thank you for being with me always.*

Day 5: When It Rains, It Pours

Do not let your hearts be troubled.
Trust in God; trust also in me.
—John 14:1

VELMA AND HARRY were looking forward
to their retirement years. They had recently
moved into a beautiful house on a hill over-
looking acres of Ponderosa pines. From the
west side of the house, they could view Pikes
Peak, the mountain that inspired "America,
the Beautiful." Mornings, they enjoyed breakfast on their redwood deck. They marveled
at the pink tint cast by the sun on the mountain's eastern slope, and it seemed to them

that every morning the snowcapped peak kissed the blue Colorado sky. Life was good!

Then tragedy struck. One night, a fatal heart attack took Harry from Velma. Devastated and alone, she struggled to rebuild her life. But it wasn't easy. She could not sing a hymn at church without choking and getting teary-eyed. A couple of times, she carried a cup of coffee to the redwood deck, but just a glimpse of Pikes Peak reminded her of the times she and Harry had enjoyed breakfast together. She missed those times terribly.

Not long after the funeral, Velma's forty-year-old daughter was diagnosed with breast cancer. Then word came from Minnesota that Velma's only brother was scheduled for open-heart surgery. Next, she learned that her soldier grandson had sustained a serious injury in a live-ammunition training exercise.

Velma was feeling like a female Job. Her emotions were in a state of turmoil, and her mental anguish was almost unbearable. She screamed at God, blaming him for allowing such horrific trouble to strike her.

Eventually, Velma accepted the fact that anger and bitterness could not improve her lot in life or alleviate her emotional pain. She surrendered her anxiety to the Lord and asked him to comfort her and her loved ones.

Christians are not exempt from turmoil, and often it seems the older we get, the harder it hits us. The senior years can bring surgeries, separation from loved ones, soaring expenses, and sagging incomes. At times, we feel that we are adrift at sea, caught in a typhoon, and on the verge of drowning. And like the disciples who literally were caught in a life-threatening storm at sea, we call out to the Lord, "Don't you care?" Then the Lord calms our troubled sea, and asks, "Why are you so afraid? Do you still have no faith?" (see Mark 4:38, 40).

We may need to wait patiently for the Lord to still our troubled waters, but we don't have to wait for him to calm our troubled hearts. His peace is only a whispered prayer away.

LORD, *I can't handle my overwhelming trials alone. I feel that you are the only One who truly understands what I am going through. Grant me wisdom, patience, and peace so I may honor you in this time of turmoil.*

Section 2 · FINANCES

Day 6: 401 KO'd

Cast but a glance at riches, and they are gone, for they will
surely sprout wings and fly off to the sky like an eagle.
—Proverbs 23:5

LIKE SO MANY Americans, Matt was putting 15 percent of his paycheck into his high-tech company's 401(k) plan, and after eighteen years it had turned into a tidy sum of money, all of which was invested in the company. He anticipated the day when he would retire, buy a set of custom-made golf clubs, and take life easy. He and his wife would not only have time for travel but also the wherewithal to stay at luxury resorts. *Uh huh*, Matt mused, *life is good now, but it's going to be even better when I retire.*

But suddenly life turned bitter, not better. The company Matt worked for fell on hard times. The company went belly-up, and so did Matt's 401(k); the company was knocked out by a below-the-belt punch delivered by an executive heavyweight. Also, Matt and hundreds of his fellow employees got knocked out—knocked out of employment.

Corporate scandals hurt not only the guilty but also the innocent and provide clear evidence that a lack of business ethics and personal morality hurts families on Walnut Street as well as financiers on Wall Street.

"The future is as bright as the promises of God." So spoke missionary Adoniram Judson more than 150 years ago. The future looked bright, not because of a swelling 401(k) account; he didn't have one. On the contrary, he had very little money, and he spent many months in a Burmese prison. His only stocks and bonds were those clamped around his feet and wrists. Yet because Adoniram believed God had promised to take care of him and reward his missionary efforts, he anticipated a bright future.

If life knocks you flat on your back, at least you will be looking up. And don't be surprised to find God reaching down to pick you up and set you on your feet again.

LORD, *true and lasting security is found only in you. May my faith always be in you and not in uncertain riches or favorable circumstances.*

Day 7: A Rational Sacrifice

For Christ died for sins once for all, the righteous
for the unrighteous, to bring you to God.
−1 Peter 3:18

DURING THE SECOND World War everyone in North America was called on to make sacrifices. The young men and women who left their homes and families to train and serve on the front lines made the obvious sacrifices. At home, less obvious ones involved organized activities to support what became known as "the war effort."

In those challenging times everyone felt the pressures of doing without something.

Most families would gather each evening around the radio and listen intently to the latest news from overseas, hoping to hear of a victorious effort or advancement by the Allied forces into enemy territory. New car production ground to a halt, and those with automobiles had to squeeze a few more miles out of the old Ford. Many other items that had always been plentiful in the past were becoming scarce. The government began to issue ration cards to give families the opportunity to purchase some goods in limited quantity.

I (Joe) remember standing in long lines with my mother, waiting for rationed food and other items to be parceled out. Some days it seemed that we just went from one line to another to purchase products. For the most part, I understood the reasons for all the waiting. It was indeed a treat to have butter, meat, and eggs, which seemed to be worth the wait. However, standing in line for more than an hour one day for a pair of nylon stockings was a bit too much for a four-year-old boy, even though my mother didn't seem to mind.

When the war ended in 1945, things immediately opened up. We were back to shopping at the local A&P grocery store, where food and other items were in good supply. Yet I haven't forgotten the lines and the rationing ... or the nylons.

When believers think of sacrifice, our minds invariably envision a cross on a hill outside Jerusalem, some two thousand years ago. There, the ultimate sacrifice took place. The Son of God gave himself for the sins of humankind.

Imagine, the One who knew no sin subjecting himself to the cruel and devastating punishment of crucifixion with all its horror. And he did so not for his friends but for his enemies.

Jesus Christ humbly and obediently paid the price we could never pay to redeem us to a righteous relationship with God.

It makes standing in line for a pound of cheese pretty insignificant.

LORD, *help us when we tend to complain about our situations to remember the enormous sacrifice you made for us and the eternal result we will enjoy together.*

Day 8: Making Ends Meet

Seek first his kingdom and his righteousness,
and all these things will be given to you as well.
—Matthew 6:33

MOST SENIORS live on a fixed income that requires constant fixing. The cost of filling up the car's gas tank is definitely high octane even when the gas is low octane. Remember when gas cost about twenty cents a gallon and an attendant pumped it, checked the oil, and also washed the windshield? The cost of heating the house seems to be going through the roof faster than smoke from the chimney. Food eats up your

Social Security allowance faster than you eat your food. And when it comes to medical and prescription costs—well, let's not even go there.

Our challenge, as seniors, is to stretch our income so that it will reach the ends that seem to keep moving farther apart. But how do we do that?

One way is to refuse to buy what we don't need. If we really don't need more clothes, even if they are marked down 50 percent at the department store, we ought to say no and save some closet space—and budget space too. If the car runs okay and doesn't pollute the air, talk back to all the new car commercials. Remember that a new car becomes a used car the minute you drive it off the dealer's lot.

Another way to get financial handles on those ends that keep moving farther apart is to conserve and consolidate. Instead of driving a mile to pick up a loaf of bread, walk! We would all be better off if we walked more and drove less. And think of the gas we would save by walking! Also, visit the grocery store less often and you will save gas. Make it a habit to shop for groceries after eating a meal. We tend to buy more when we are hungry.

If you have the health and stamina to work part-time, why not give it a try? A number of companies are discovering how smart it is to hire older workers. It seems we seniors have a good work ethic and demonstrate company loyalty. If you can't work away from home, maybe you can work from home. Make an inventory of your skills. Can you prepare taxes, write articles, babysit, teach music, or turn a hobby into a cottage industry? You may be pleasantly surprised to learn that people will pay for your services.

Finally, trust the Lord to provide all that you need. He has promised to do so, and he never breaks a promise. Assume the positive attitude of the believer who commented, "I may be living from hand to mouth, but it is the Lord's hand and my mouth."

LORD, *I trust you to provide for all my needs. Protect me from needless worry. Give me the wisdom to make good financial decisions, the discipline to carry them out, and the courage to attempt new ventures.*

Day 9: Out of the Blue

My God will meet all your needs according
to his glorious riches in Christ Jesus.
—Philippians 4:19

WHEN EDNA CAME home from the hospital she knew things were going to be much different than before. Her family had fixed a comfortable space for her in a finished attic room in their small house, and although far from spacious, this was where she would be spending most of her time.

After a few weeks, Edna began feeling somewhat lonely in her little room. Of course there was the TV and her radio, but neither afforded much companionship. Because most of her family worked, she faced many hours alone each day. Not that she complained. She knew many seniors who were a lot worse off.

Then one day at noon, she heard the bells. At first she thought it was one of the ice-cream trucks that regularly drove through her neighborhood. But, no, these bells were playing hymns—hymns she hadn't heard since she went to Sunday school as a child. It was wonderful. Just as she began to hum along, the bells stopped! Then, six hours later, they began playing again. The next day, the same thing happened. Precisely at noon, a whole new raft of melodies flooded her lonely room, bringing encouragement and joy. She had to find out where they were coming from. She asked her family to inquire and learned that the big church on the corner two blocks away had recently installed a new carillon.

The next day, Edna called the church and spoke to the minister. She told him how much the beautiful bells meant to her. He thanked her for her call and made an appointment to visit her. Afterward, the minister put Edna on his weekly visitation list, and she began looking forward to each Tuesday when he would arrive with words of comfort and cheer. He would read Scripture and lead in prayer and then just listen to Edna talk about her past, of growing up in a small town, and about her marriage and children. When it was time for him to leave, Edna would say, "Someday you'll be repaid for all your kindness."

A few months later, Edna died. At the reading of her will, and to the utter surprise of the minister, she had left him, personally, over a quarter of a million dollars. Although the family contested, the courts upheld the bequest and eventually Edna's wishes were honored. The minister, being a man of integrity, immediately endorsed the gift to the church, which, at the time, was going through some financial hardships.

In the end, Edna's generosity meant that her beloved bells would continue to ring out the good news of the gospel in that neighborhood for many years to come.

LORD, *help me to realize that you can meet any need in my life. Amen.*

Day 10: Reverse Mortgages

Do not store up for yourselves treasures on earth,
where moth and rust destroy, and where thieves break in
and steal. But store up for yourselves treasures in heaven.
—Matthew 6:19–20

HAVE YOU OWNED a high-mileage car and wished you could take a big number of miles off the odometer? Maybe you considered putting the car in reverse and driving backward for a while. But you were smart enough to realize that driving in reverse was not the way to go; it just wouldn't get rid of those unwanted miles.

When it comes to personal income,

though, one possible way to go forward is to put your house in reverse. Lending agencies are now offering reverse mortgages that actually pay homeowners a monthly amount, providing them with a steady income. Of course, if a homeowner decides to sell his home in ten years, the lending agency will collect its share of the sale money, depending upon how much it has paid the homeowner over the course of those ten years. Also, the owner must pay closing costs and other fees when he takes out a reverse mortgage, and every dollar the bank pays the homeowner is a dollar less for the homeowner's heirs. There is the risk, too, that the homeowner will outlive the reverse mortgage and no longer have equity in the house. So count the cost before you count the gain.

Joanne had been a widow for several years, and she struggled to make ends meet on a fixed income. As soon as she thought the ends would meet, the utility company, tax assessor, and oil companies seemed to team up and move the ends farther apart. Then Joanne heard about reverse mortgages. Her son and daughters told her they wanted her to live comfortably rather than struggle to own her house outright so they would inherit it someday. So Joanne took out a reverse mortgage that would augment her Social Security income. Now she doesn't have to set the thermostat at 64 degrees, eat Spam three times a week, and drive her car only to church and to the doctor. Life is looking pretty good to Joanne.

Each of us must assess the worth of our possessions and decide what kind of lifestyle the Lord wants us to maintain. A modest income that allows us to live free of financial worry is probably what most of us desire. But what kind of inheritance do we want to leave to our children and grandchildren? They might not want our house, so we might want to consider a reverse mortgage if we need to beef up our income. However, whether we live on little or much, we can leave a rich spiritual inheritance to our beneficiaries. By leading a life of faith and godliness, we can bless our children and grandchildren and, at the same time, store up treasures in heaven.

LORD, *I trust you for my daily needs and thank you for providing for me faithfully through the years. Lead me in paths of righteousness. Fill me with your love until it overflows to all who know me. May I leave my heirs a godly inheritance, and may I store up true wealth in heaven.*

Day II: Who's That Knocking at My Door?

Food gained by fraud tastes sweet to a man,
but he ends up with a mouth full of gravel.
—Proverbs 20:17

EACH YEAR CON artists swindle thousands of senior citizens out of their hard-earned money. And with the rising cost of living reflected in health care, taxes, utilities, groceries, and gasoline, who can afford to kiss their money good-bye?

Con artists do what legitimate businessmen would never dream of doing. For example, a con artist may knock on a senior citizen's door and introduce himself as a roofer. His pitch (a sales pitch, not a roof pitch) may go like this:

"Good morning, sir. That was quite a wind-storm last night. I represent the No-Flap Roofing Company. My partner and I just finished a big job ahead of schedule and thought we might be able to do some small jobs at a bargain price before going back home down-state. From the street I could see that the wind knocked some of your shingles loose, and a few are damaged. If you like, I can fix those shingles tomorrow for only five hundred dollars. I can pick up matching shingles at the supplier tomorrow morning and put them on for you in the afternoon. At the same time, I'll secure the loose shingles with roofing cement and nails. My price is about half what you would pay someone else, and I'm sure you don't want to climb a ladder and do the job yourself. All I need from you today is an okay and a check for three hundred dollars made out to cash so I can buy the materials."

Of course, once the phony roofer has a check, he checks out. He becomes a no-show, and the roofing job has become a con job.

Better safe than sorry. Consult the Better Business Bureau before letting any person or company take your money. Never agree to any repairs or improvements without a contract. And be sure to read the contract carefully. Make sure it includes details about the work to be performed and the materials to be used, and that it gives the completion date. Then both you and the contractor should sign it.

The building trades are not the only breeding grounds for con artists. Unfortunately, unscrupulous seekers of fast and easy money worm their way into almost every vocation and profession. Even religion has its share of con artists, not-so-reverend reverends who deceive their followers in order to deepen their own pockets. They promise to pray for the elderly but only prey on them. They offer the hope of health and prosperity in return for donations. Some swindle gullible fans out of their homes and life savings. Jesus warned us to "watch out for false prophets. They come to you in sheep's clothing … inwardly they are ferocious wolves" (Matt. 7:15). And the apostle Paul blasted these religious charlatans. He charged, "Their destiny is destruction, their god is their stomach, and their glory is in their shame. Their mind is on earthly things" (Phil. 3:19).

Of course, the best way to recognize a counterfeit is to know the real thing. No wonder Paul instructed each of us to be an approved workman "who correctly handles the word of truth" (2 Tim. 2:15).

LORD, *as I read and study your Word, help me know the truth so well that even the most appealing lies will not deceive me.*

Section 3 · FAMILY

Day 12: Grandchildren Are Great, But . . .

There is a time for everything,
and a season for every activity under heaven.
—Ecclesiastes 3:1

"LET ME SHOW you some pictures of the grandchildren. There's Susie. Isn't she adorable? She's wearing the dress I gave her for Easter. She has her mother's smile, and everyone says she has my eyes and nose. She will be six next month.

"This one's Billy. He's riding a pony at the county fair. He sure liked that pony. Look how he's flashing a big grin and waving at me. He's always such a ham for the camera! He just turned four a couple of days before this picture was taken."

Sound familiar? Chances are ten out of ten every grandparent has shown pictures of the grandchildren and gushed about those kids that are a little smarter and better looking than most other kids.

But if you are like most grandparents, you're more than a little relieved that the grandchildren are not your full-time responsibility. If they were, you might have to double your daily intake of Geritol and vitamins. All you have to do is spend a little time with them once in a while to discover how tiring the experience can be. Grandmas know that playing dolls with little Susie is okay for fifteen minutes, but exhaustion sets in after a couple of hours of dressing, undressing, rocking, and walking dolls, plus combing their hair and holding endless make-believe conversations. Grandpas who play ball with their little future Hall of Famer can hardly wait to retreat to "the bench" so they can rest an aching back or sore knees or a tight shoulder or a nagging hip—or all of the aforementioned.

Yep, being a grandparent isn't for sissies, but there's no shame in uttering a sigh of relief when you give the grandkids back to their parents. In Ecclesiastes, wise King Solomon commented, "There is a time for everything" (3:1). In most people's lives, there is a time for parenting and a time for grandparenting; and thankfully, they are two different times.

On the whole, it doesn't take much to please us grandparents. A whispered "I love you, Grandma (or Grandpa)" or a warm hug brings a smile to our faces, a warm feeling to our hearts, and even little tears of joy to our eyes. Our grandkids have gentle ways of making us glad we are their grandparents.

But the privilege of being a grandparent joins hands with responsibility. We have a duty to show them God's love and what it means to love him in return. Maybe, just maybe, we can do that whenever we read a Bible story to a grandchild, throw a ball to Timmy, dress a doll with Tammy, take Cory to the zoo, watch a kids' video with Keri, or eat pizza with Josh.

Wouldn't it be great if our grandkids saw no difference between WWJD (What Would Jesus Do?) and WWGD (What Would Grandma or Grandpa Do?)?

LORD, *help me to take every opportunity to enjoy my grandchildren and to show them your love.*

Day 13: Growing Old Isn't So Bad After All

Forgetting what is behind and straining toward what is ahead,
I press on toward the goal to win the prize for which God
has called me heavenward in Christ Jesus.
—*Philippians 3:13–14*

RECENTLY, I (Jim) read a statement that flipped many, many mental calendars back to my growing-up years. Here it is: "When you are dissatisfied and would like to go back to your youth, think of Algebra."

Frankly, I don't get dissatisfied very often, just occasionally. Dissatisfaction strikes when I have to wait thirty minutes in a dinky cubicle at the doctor's office with nothing to read except a hazardous waste warning on a trashcan. It strikes on a golf course, too, when I miss a two-foot putt. How can I miss such a short putt 95 percent of the time? But if I had to sit in Algebra class again or live through some other experiences from my youth, sitting in a cubicle or missing short putts wouldn't seem so bad.

You remember what it was like to grow up in the 1930s and '40s, don't you? Nobody drove you to school; you walked. School buses didn't exist. Neither did snow days. And when you were at school, you had to respect your teachers—maybe even fear them. Teachers weren't fun, and they didn't feel obligated to make learning fun. Nor were they particularly concerned about our self-image. What mattered to them was that we learned what we were supposed to learn and behaved as we were supposed to behave. If we failed to learn, we were held back without regard for how we felt about it.

If we failed to behave, we were paddled—at school and at home.

After school, we had to do homework or chores or both. Television was practically unheard of, and video games hadn't even made it to the world of Buck Rogers. There wasn't even a McDonald's or a mall to hang out at. So we either played in the neighborhood or watched Mom bake a pie.

When we were old enough to work part-time, we received about twenty cents an hour. A heavy snowfall sent us into the frigid air with a shovel in hand. We knocked on neighbors' doors and volunteered to clear their sidewalks for a quarter.

Oh, living in the 1930s and '40s wasn't totally bad, of course. We learned to respect our elders and to value life. We developed character and learned the value of a nickel. Nobody pushed drugs at us or tried to get us to go along on a drive-by shooting. And if we went to Sunday school, we all memorized Scripture from the same Bible version.

Yes, I would rather live today than return to the days of my youth. The opportunities to serve the Lord and to pass on a godly heritage to the grandkids sure beat sitting in school and trying to figure out what $(x+y3)-18$ equals.

* * *

LORD, *I thank you for the privilege of being alive in the twenty-first century. May I consider all my past experiences guideposts instead of hitching posts.*

Day 14: On the Road Again

I remember the days of long ago; I meditate on all your
works and consider what your hands have done.
—Psalm 143:5

ENTERTAINERS SEEM to have a fascination with roads. Willie Nelson sings, "On the road again, just can't wait to get on the road again." The late John Denver's "Country Roads" was a big hit. And remember those Bing Crosby/Bob Hope road movies? From 1939 to 1952, Bing and Bob found success on the road to Singapore, the road to Zanzibar, the road to Morocco, the road to Utopia, the road to Rio, and the road to Bali.

During their fiftieth year of marriage, Matt and Susan decided to visit every apartment or house they had lived in from the day they returned from their honeymoon to the present. Their main object was to compile a scrapbook of memories for each of their children. It would include photos of each residence, a description of the location, and brief paragraphs of memories associated with that chapter of their life together. They knew they were embarking on a "Mission Almost Impossible." After all, they had lived in forty-one places from California to Mississippi. But off they went, traveling by car and singing from place to place, "On the Road Again."

Revisiting former residences may not be for every senior, but Matt and Susan would tell you they had a blast and were able to give each of their children a scrapbook of memories that will last a lifetime.

Thousands of enjoyable moments and events fill our memory bank. But, like deposits in a regular bank, they serve us best when we use them.

The Lord is pleased when we reach into our memory bank for reminders of his love and goodness. Thousands of such images are on deposit there, aren't they? We recall how he restored our health, found us a job, put food on our table, provided us with a comfortable place to live, brought good friends into our life, took care of our children—even let us score an occasional birdie on the golf course. Maybe a stroll down memory lane to revisit incidents of his love and goodness is just the ticket to wonderful senior moments of grace.

LORD, *I remember your love and goodness, and I thank you for all the deeds you have performed in my life. May I never forget how blessed I am.*

Day 15: Raising Kids
the Second Time Around

Even when I am old and gray, do not forsake me,
O God, till I declare your power to the next generation,
your might to all who are to come.
—*Psalm 71:18*

"NOW THAT the kids are married and have
kids of their own, let's take that cruise we've
always talked about."

"Well, Honey, we did it. We raised Mark,
Jill, and Jessica, helped them get through
college, and spent a ton of money on their
weddings. Now *they* are finding out what

parenting is all about. Now we can kick back and take life easy."

Hold the phone! Statements like these have returned to bite seniors. In the United States alone, more than six million children live with their grandparents or other relatives who are not their parents.

In many cases, parents are unable or unwilling to provide for their children. So they turn the kids over to Grandma and Grandpa—in some situations, only to one grandparent because the grandparent is divorced or a widow or widower.

For those on a fixed income or battling health problems, raising kids the second time around is about as unsettling as riding a roller coaster after forcing down too much Chicago-style pizza.

So what's a grandparent to do?

First, open your heart to your grandkids. They are probably struggling with feelings of rejection, loneliness, and uncertainty. They need you! Your love, patience, and wise guidance can protect them from self-blame and despair.

Second, open your heart to the Lord. He cares about your situation, and he has promised to be with you, to sustain you, and to supply inexhaustible grace. When you feel like you have reached the end of your rope—and you will—recall that his arms are underneath you (see Deut. 33:27).

Third, open your directory of community resources. You may be pleasantly surprised to find a support group and/or financial, educational, and other resources. Some communities supply grandparents with books, brochures, and articles on parenting.

Fourth, open your life to new opportunities to grow. Grandkids can expand your world. Their educational endeavors, participation in sports, and experiences with technology can introduce you to new friends, new ideas, and new skills. By stretching yourself physically, socially, and intellectually, you will probably enjoy better health and greater fulfillment.

Finally, open your relationship with the Lord to the observation and questioning of your grandkids. Be a good example. Let them see the benefits of following Christ. Let them ask questions about your faith. Use even unplanned moments to teach them how to live.

Raising kids the second time around may not be on any grandparent's wish list, but if the experience falls to you, you just may enjoy it more than the first time.

LORD, *if the task of raising my grandkids falls to me, help me to raise them well as a service to you—and to them.*

Section 4 · HEALTH

Day 16: Catching Some Rays

I am the light of the world. Whoever follows me will never walk in darkness, but will have the light of life.
—John 8:12

COLD, GRAY days didn't bother us when we were kids, did they? We welcomed the opportunity to play outdoors any day of the week, under almost any conditions. Television was in its infancy back then, and watching Uncle Milty wasn't nearly as appealing as playing softball or hide-and-seek with the neighborhood kids. "Put a sweater or coat on before you go outside," Mom would tell us, but we didn't always follow her instructions. We would feel warm despite a lack of sunshine.

What has happened to our body's thermostat in the mature years? It doesn't seem to work the way it did when we were kids. If we step outdoors on a gray, sixty-degree day without a sweater or a coat, we shiver and pray for sunshine.

Actually, the older we grow the more we need to step into the sunshine. Studies have shown that direct sunlight absorbed through the skin stimulates the body's production of vitamin D. However, more than half of all adults over sixty-five are vitamin D deficient. Twenty minutes of exposure to the sun several times a week gives the body an adequate supply of vitamin D, which in turn helps the body build stronger bones and protects against heart disease, certain cancers, rheumatoid arthritis, and multiple sclerosis.

So make it a goal to catch some rays when the sun shines on your neighborhood!

Exposure to the Son, though, is infinitely more important than exposure to the sun that rises and sets every day. The sun improves the quality of our physical life, but Jesus, the Son of God, gives eternal life to all who believe in him. Further, he provides a quality of life that those who live in spiritual darkness do not have. Psalm 84:11 cites the benefits of walking in the Son's light: "For the LORD God is a sun and shield; the LORD bestows favor and honor; no good thing does he withhold from those whose walk is blameless."

Let's open up our hearts and let the Son shine in!

LORD, *help me to walk today and every day in fellowship with your Son, Jesus Christ, and may I reflect his light to others.*

Day 17: Contentment

I have learned to be content whatever the circumstances.
—Philippians 4:11

RECENTLY, WHILE spending some time in the hospital, I (Joe) became acquainted with a very wonderful lady. Margaret was one of the nurses assigned to the unit where I was recovering. The first time I saw her I was impressed by her sprightly manner. She would come into the room from time to time to record my blood pressure, pulse, and temperature. She always spoke a pleasant word as she went about her business. Margaret appeared to be about sixty years old, but her bouncy presence and sunny disposition portrayed a woman of much younger years. Imagine my surprise when I found out she had just turned eighty-three!

I had to find out more about Margaret.

One day as she was finishing her duties, I told her how much her positive attitude encouraged me. She paused for a moment, thanked me, and then told her incredible story.

Margaret and her husband had two sons, the oldest of whom had died suddenly at the young age of thirty-seven. Depressed and despondent, her husband withdrew to the point where he just gave up on life. He continuously sat in his chair, stared into space, and died six months later. What made this story even more touching was that her other son died at age forty-seven.

I asked her what kept her going through all this tragedy. Without blinking an eye, she replied, "My faith. You see, I figured there must be a reason the Lord took away the people who were most precious to me. And then it dawned on me. He wanted me to be in a position to be able to take care of a whole lot of people. Now my patients have become, in a real sense, my family, and I love to care for them."

What a remarkable person. Margaret had every reason, humanly speaking, to retreat to a life of discouragement and self-pity. Instead, she kept a heavenly perspective, saw beyond her circumstances, and enthusiastically grasped the God-given opportunity to serve him and others.

In the Scriptures we have the encouraging words of the apostle Paul regarding contentment. After writing Philippians 4:11, he continued: "I know what it is to be in need, and I know what it is to have plenty. I have learned the secret of being content in any and every situation, whether well fed or hungry, whether living in plenty or in want" (v. 12). Then he revealed the secret: "I can do everything through him who gives me strength" (v. 13).

The thing that is so interesting about Paul's words on contentment is that when he wrote them he was under house arrest in Rome, chained day and night to a Roman guard. Now, if Paul could be content in that situation and Margaret could find contentment during her darkest hour, it must mean that the Lord can indeed bring victory to us no matter what we're going through.

FATHER, *thank you for your faithful presence during our toughest trials and the confidence that you will bring the sweetest victory to those who trust you.*

Day 18: Eat Smart, Be Smart

How sweet are your words to my taste,
sweeter than honey to my mouth! I gain understanding
from your precepts; therefore I hate every wrong path.
—Psalm 119:103–104

FOR YEARS we have heard that fish is brain food, but we might ask why the fish got caught if they were so smart. Now the Galachia Center on Aging at Kansas State University claims that mental alertness and good nutrition are linked. If we maintain a varied diet with fruits, vegetables, whole grains, and proper amounts of protein, and cut back on sugar and fat, we may stay alert and healthy for a long time.

For most of us mature adults, shifting our eating habits may not be a simple matter, though. When we were kids, we were taught to eat everything Mom put on our plate. Often that meant finishing a big pile of mashed potatoes and gravy, gobbling down the last ounce of corned beef hash, and swallowing what remained of a glob of buttered lima beans. A big slice of bread always accompanied dinner, and a meal wasn't complete without a slice of pie or cake or both.

Yes, we ate plenty when we were kids. We didn't count calories, but our mental alertness wasn't so bad. After all, we could count numbers without the aid of a calculator. Also, we knew how to spell and recite important dates in history. Our diet may have been haywire, but our discipline was A-OK. And we've made it this far in life without existing on greens and grapefruit. So why change our eating habits now?

The answer is simple: Life is too valuable to let starches, fats, and sugar rob us of our best years. We need to keep our bodies as fit as possible and our minds as sharp as possible. We want to be at our best as we serve the Lord.

Do we need to read Romans 12:1–2 again as a reminder that God wants us to dedicate both body and mind to him? He wants to use our hands, feet, mouth, ears, eyes, heart, and mind in his service. We do not know how many days, months, or years remain for us to serve him, but we do know his servants are immortal until their life's work is done. So pass the veggies, please!

LORD, *I dedicate my mind to you. Help me stay mentally focused on what is true, noble, right, pure, lovely, admirable, excellent, and praiseworthy, so that my thoughts may produce deeds that honor you.*

Day 19: I'm Gonna Live Till I Die

So here I am today, eighty-five years old! I am still
as strong today as the day Moses sent me out; I'm just as
vigorous to go out to battle now as I was then.
—Joshua 14:10–11

CALEB SPOKE the words quoted above, and he backed them up by chasing giants from Mount Hebron. Unlike Caleb, most of us would be happy to chase a golf ball around a course at eighty-five and leave the giant-chasing business to a younger generation. Giant chasing may be more exciting, but aching joints and limp muscles are simply no match for giants.

Reaching age eighty-five may soon be only a minor accomplishment, thanks to an ever-increasing variety of prescription drugs and a growing number of opportunities to exercise. We can swallow a pill to combat high blood pressure, another to lower cholesterol, another to reduce bone loss, another to stabilize our sugar, and one more to ward off depression. The depression may strike hardest when we get billed for the pills. Having downed a plethora of pills, we can go to a gym and burn off unwanted calories. It's all quite a price to pay for increased longevity!

The average life span of an American born today is 77.2 years. Advances in medicine and health may quickly drive the average to one hundred by the end of this century. The U.S. Census Bureau reports that in 2050 twenty-one million Americans will be over the age of eighty-five.

But what quality of life will accompany a larger quantity of years? Who wants to live long if his or her life seems insignificant?

Well, for Christians the news is fantastic. Living life in obedience to God brings a sense of significance, joy, and even excitement. There is no better way to travel to the heavenly Zion than in fellowship with the Lord. The psalmist declared, "Blessed are those whose strength is in you, who have set their hearts on pilgrimage" (Ps. 84:5).

So take those pills, ride that stationary bike—and serve the Lord. That way you will live—really live—till you die.

LORD, *I want all my remaining years to be quality years, so I am dedicating them and myself to you.*

Day 20: Laughter: Free Medicine for Body and Soul

A cheerful heart is good medicine,
but a crushed spirit dries up the bones.
—Proverbs 17:22

MOST CHURCHES include a seniors' group that meets regularly for fellowship and activities. They may go by the name of Keenagers or Seasoned Saints or the Young at Heart Club or the Elderberries or some other moniker, but they all have three things in common: faith, an appetite for home-cooked food, and a great sense of humor.

Now, an appetite can have either good or bad health consequences. You be the judge. Consider what's on the menu at most senior potlucks: fruit salad, five-bean salad, lasagna, fried chicken, mashed potatoes, sausages, heavily buttered corn, dumplings, pecan pie with ice cream, big chunks of fudge, and thirty or forty other high-caloric choices. When it comes to choosing food, many seniors choose everything available.

Of course, faith has only good consequences. It gives seniors an optimistic outlook and a sense that God is watching over them.

A sense of humor is good for us too. It leads to laughter, and laughter lifts our spirits, fights facial wrinkles, relieves stress, lowers blood pressure, and strengthens our diaphragm and abdominal, respiratory, facial, leg, and back muscles. Laughing a hundred times is equal to ten minutes on the rowing machine or fifteen minutes on an exercise bike. Although some wonder drugs make us wonder what's going to happen next, laughter acts as a reliable medicine. We always feel better after a good laugh. Plus, laughter is a free medicine!

In our politically correct era, it isn't acceptable to joke about race, gender, or nationality, but seniors can joke about their age and physical conditions with impunity. And they aren't about to give that up.

One senior commented, "I'm sure everything I can't find is in a secure place."

Another mused, "I'm wondering, if you're only as old as you feel, how could I be alive at 150?"

"I'm wrinkled, saggy, and lumpy, but that's just my left leg," another volunteered.

If laughter keeps us young, today's seniors must surely be thirty-nine and holding!

Jesus promised that walking in his ways would bring happiness and joy. After teaching his disciples about humility and serving others, he said, "Now that you know these things, you will be blessed [happy] if you do them" (John 13:17). He also told them if they remained in his love and obeyed his commands, his joy would remain in them and their joy would be complete (see 15:10–11).

Don't let disobedience or "Father Time" rob you of happiness and joy. Surround yourself with others who love the Lord. Encourage one another to obey the Lord, and laugh together. Some of your jokes may be old, but you may have forgotten them.

Just one word of caution: Don't laugh too hard on a stomach full of lasagna, pecan pie, and fudge!

LORD, *I thank you that a cheerful heart is good medicine and free, too. It has no adverse side effects, and I can't overdose on it. May I always follow you cheerfully. Please use me today to bring happiness and laughter to others.*

Day 21: This Old House

Therefore, I urge you, brothers, in view of God's mercy,
to offer your bodies as living sacrifices, holy and pleasing
to God—this is your spiritual act of worship.
—Romans 12:1

IN THE 1950S, Christians were singing "This Old House," a song written by Stuart Hamlin. It compared a believer's aging body to a house whose windows, floors, and doors were wearing out. But in that song, Stuart said he didn't have time to fix the shingles, fix the floor, oil the hinges, or mend the windowpanes. "I won't need this house much longer," he wrote. "I'm getting ready to meet the saints."

Stuart was on to something. This old house, the human body, leaves much to be desired. The older it gets, the more it sags, squeaks, staggers, slumbers, shutters, and shakes. We visit doctors and pharmacies more often than we visit grocery stores, and pills cram our medicine cabinets more than commuters cram a New York subway train at 5:00 p.m. on Friday. Most three-year-olds can tie their shoelaces faster than we can, and they can consume a biggie order of french fries faster than we can swallow a glass of Metamucil.

And those slick, one-pill or one-ointment cure-all commercials don't help at all. You know the kind: Grandma can't play ball with Billy because her arthritic shoulder is killing her. But after rubbing just one dab of that no-smell Wonderlube on her shoulder, she turns into a pitching ace. Billy is ecstatic; he thinks Grandma might win the Cy Young Award.

Of course, some medicinal aids can help alleviate our pain, but this old house will never return to mint condition. We can slow the aging process, but we can't stop it. Nevertheless, the old house has served us well for decades and will be our residence until our final moving day.

According to 1 Corinthians 6:19–20, the Christian should honor God with his body because it is a temple of the Holy Spirit. The Christian's body is also referred to as a house (see 2 Cor. 5:1 KJV). No matter how tired or stressed our "house" may be, we ought to maintain it as well as we can. Following a proper diet, getting adequate rest, and exercising regularly are just a few important ways to show respect for the body as God's possession and the Spirit's residence. Following our doctor's orders and taking our prescribed medications consistently are two additional ways.

We can honor God with our bodies by speaking kind, loving words; by listening to a neighbor's concerns; by talking about the goodness of the Lord; by hugging a grandchild;

by extending a helping hand to the needy; by walking into a patient's hospital or nursing home room and offering a smile; and by bending our knees in prayer on behalf of others.

We may not need this old house much longer, but until we vacate it, let's take care of it and honor its builder.

LORD, *may my hands, feet, lips, and ears honor you, and may my heart beat with love for you and others until you post my final moving day from this old house.*

Day 22: Too Soon Old and Too Late Smart!

If any of you lacks wisdom, he should ask God,
who gives generously to all without finding fault,
and it will be given to him.
—James 1:5

IF YOU VISIT a gift shop in Amish country, you may find a plaque that reads, "We get too soon old and too late smart." How true that is!

Our generation is pretty smart, but we don't have unlimited time to apply what we have learned. We are smart enough to know:

- It's better to spend time with the family than with the boss.

- It's better to forgive and forget than to harbor a grudge.
- A chip on the shoulder is too heavy a load to carry.
- Hugging our loved ones strengthens our arms—and our heart.
- Money can buy everything that doesn't last.
- The Amish are right: Kissing doesn't last; good cooking does!
- Grandchildren keep us young—and tired.
- Going into debt isn't worth the effort it takes to get out of debt.
- The best things in life aren't things.
- Who we have is worth far more than what we have.
- Time flies faster than a 747.
- A $2.75 slice of pie today tastes no better than a 35¢ slice of pie did forty years ago.
- A simple meal with friends is a profound pleasure.

- A person wrapped up in himself makes a very small package.
- The more we give of ourselves the bigger we grow.
- "Lasting peace" is a term used between wars and military conflicts.
- The world has become a neighborhood but not a brotherhood.

It seems even King Solomon, Israel's wisest king, wasn't so smart at times. First Kings 11:3 reports that he had seven hundred wives (dumb!) and three hundred concubines (dumber!) who led him away from God (dumbest!). It's a good thing Valentine's Day wasn't celebrated back then. Buying cards and gifts for all those wives and lovers would have drained Israel's coffers.

In the book of Ecclesiastes, Solomon traces his journey for the meaning of life. He tells us he pored over tons of books as he searched for wisdom. He tried pleasure, wealth, possessions, music, and entrepreneurship but found no meaning in any of those things. Finally, he focused on God and found lasting significance and fulfillment in him. Summing up his discovery, Solomon counseled, "Remember your Creator in the days of your youth, before the days of trouble come and the years approach when you will say, 'I find no pleasure in them'" (Eccl. 12:1).

Solomon wasn't Amish, but it seems he was saying, "We get too soon old and too late smart."

LORD, *I ask you to crown my senior years with wisdom. Time passes too quickly to waste precious moments chasing frivolous pleasures and empty dreams. May what I put into the hours of each day amount to far more than the number of hours I put in.*

Section 5 · ACTIVENESS

Day 23: Be a Grandfriend

Come, my children, listen to me;
I will teach you the fear of the LORD.
—*Psalm 34:11*

SPONSORED BY school districts, the grandfriend program invites capable volunteers to tutor learners in the classroom. A grandfatherly or grandmotherly person pulls up a chair beside an early-elementary-aged student and helps him improve his reading, writing, and math skills. In the process, Taylor gets a better handle on the three Rs, and his grandfriend gets a better handle on his self-worth. Both get a better handle on the fact that generations separated by decades can bond given the opportunity.

A similar bonding between kids and grandfriends can take place in one's neighborhood. Shayne, age ten, and his brother Cole, age seven, enjoy playing Scrabble with their sixty-something Christian neighbors. Not only do the boys get a chance to use the fancy-schmancy Scrabble board Shayne received as a Christmas gift, they also learn from their grandfriends how to rack up game points. As they discuss what's taking place at school—good and bad—they learn that their grandfriends are good listeners and helpful counselors. Perhaps best of all, they learn that sixty-something people are pretty cool.

Ken, an eighty-year-old greeter at his church, welcomes every child by name, and nearly every child gives him a big hug and a smile. If you look around your church's Sunday school, don't be surprised to find sixty-somethings teaching pre-schoolers or third-graders or some other class of youngsters. They love their students, and the students love them.

Jesus' disciples didn't see any point in letting kids visit Jesus. So they rebuked those who brought the children to Jesus (see Matt. 19:13). However, Jesus put a quick stop to the disciples' action: "Let the little children come to me ... for the kingdom of heaven belongs to such as these" (v. 14). Then he put his hands on them and blessed them (see v. 15; Mark 10:16).

Doesn't it seem to you that being a grandfriend to little kids must surely bring a smile to Jesus' face?

LORD, *so many kids are afraid to talk to adults, but if you give me the opportunity to be a grandfriend, I will help kids see that adults can be kind, loving, and helpful. In all that I say and do, I will try to help them see you.*

Day 24: Fitting In

And you also were included in Christ when you heard
the word of truth, the gospel of your salvation.
—Ephesians 1:13

HOW WELL does that old dress fit you? You know, the one you wore on your honeymoon? Or, if you are a man, how well does that suit fit you—the one that's been hanging in the closet for the past ten years?

A little snug in places?

Not to worry; it's out of style anyhow, isn't it?

Do you sometimes feel like an old dress or an old suit? Does it seem that you just don't fit the times or fit in with the younger crowd? When your grandkids rave about Mario Brothers and DVDs, you think they are talking about a twenty-first-century set of Marx brothers in underwear. When your kids talk about updating Windows, you think they are going to replace the house windows. You think TV sitcoms are silly, movie endings make no sense, and modern music resembles the sound of a steamroller running over a thousand metal trash cans. You wonder what happened to the good old days when restaurant personnel addressed customers as "ma'am" and "sir."

And what happened to plain old coffee? It tasted fine, didn't it? Why did somebody have to make ordering coffee so complicated? It must be that giving coffee fancy names justifies the $2.75-a-cup price. How can a senior possibly fit in with coffee shop yuppies who order something like a cappuccino or a frappuccino or a caramel latte or a mocha grande or an espresso? Why do they give coffee names that sound like Mafia figures? You feel like a fossil when you ask for a plain cup of coffee, don't you?

Yes, it is hard to fit in sometimes, but at least we are still around to meet the challenge! Fortunately, if we have trusted in Jesus as Savior, we always fit in with him. He is our best friend and confidant at all times and in all situations. Change may be whirling around us, but Jesus "is the same yesterday and today and forever" (Heb. 13:8).

That old dress or suit may not fit us any longer, but our relationship with Jesus can be a perfect fit today and always.

LORD, *sometimes I don't fit in, but you love me just as I am. All may change, but you do not change. You are ever faithful, true, patient, and kind. May my relationship with you fit your expectations today and always.*

Day 25: Jump, Run, or Walk, but Don't Talk to the TV

The bolts of your gates will be iron and bronze, and your
strength will equal your days.
—Deuteronomy 33:25

GERONIMO! Former president George H. W. Bush celebrated his eightieth birthday June 13, 2004, by parachuting thirteen thousand feet from an airplane under the watchful care of the Golden Knights, a U.S. Army parachute team. Apparently, Barbara Bush didn't watch. Perhaps she wasn't altogether pleased with her husband's decision to jump. Nevertheless, the forty-first president of the United States landed safely and commented that the jump was wonderful. He enjoyed the speed and freedom of falling through the air, and he said he might jump again when he turns eighty-five.

Few, if any, of us will celebrate our eightieth or eighty-first birthday by parachuting, but we can all profit from the advice Mr. Bush offered after his jump. He said seniors should get out and enjoy life instead of sitting and talking to the TV. That makes sense. Trying to hold a conversation with a TV is about as enjoyable and productive as trying to receive messages from outer space by pressing your ear to a fence post.

To stay physically active, we ought to walk or run or work out at a gym or do aquatic exercises or stretch or play golf or do whatever it takes to draw oxygen into the lungs and keep the heart pumping and the joints lubricating. If we stay active, our best years of Christian service may lie ahead.

At age eighty-five, Caleb, Joshua's right-hand officer, boldly asked Joshua for a new challenge. He knew God had kept him alive and given him past victories, so he believed God would grant him success in a venture that he was eager to embrace. He wanted to rout adversarial giants from Mount Hebron and take possession of it (see Josh. 14:6–12).

Joshua granted Caleb's request (see v. 13). Caleb possessed his prize, and gave his daughter land rich with springwater (see 15:13–19).

You and I can do better than talk to the TV. We can still fight battles for the Lord and bless others with springs of living water.

LORD, *I don't want to rust out. I want to stay active as long as life remains. I want to serve you and enrich the lives of family members and friends. Help me to reach every goal you set before me.*

Day 26: Life Begins at Any Age

I can do everything through him who gives me strength.
—Philippians 4:13

NEXT TIME you order a chicken breast—original or extra crispy—a side of mashed potatoes, and a side of baked beans at KFC, consider this fact: Harlan Sanders started the Kentucky Fried Chicken chain of restaurants when he was sixty-six. Sure, a younger person could have concocted the "secret blend of eleven herbs and spices," but only the white-haired, white-suited, sixty-six-year-old colonel took the chicken by the neck and launched a successful nationwide chain of "finger-lickin' good" food. Starting in Corbin, Kentucky, he signed up five restaurants. Four years later, he ruled the roost with over two hundred franchises. Ten years later, he sold his interest in the company for two million dollars.

Take a lesson from the Colonel: Life can begin at any age. We shouldn't let ambition and productivity die before we do.

When I (Jim) was sixteen, I took a week's leave of absence from high school and worked my father's bread route so he could drive to Ottawa, Canada, in response to a medical emergency. My grandmother had suffered a stroke, and the doctors predicted she would die within several days. However, Grandma was a bit contrary by nature, and I think she took great pleasure in contradicting her doctors. Not only did she not die within a few days, she lived another fifteen years and used those additional years to pursue a new hobby—landscape painting.

Grandma's paintings were actually very

good, and our family seized the opportunity to refer to her as Grandma Moses.

You and I may not launch a chain of restaurants or become creators of fine art, but we can turn our creativity toward pursuits that keep us young and stretch our horizons. Continuing education opportunities abound in most communities and include almost everything from computers to ceramics to German to gourmet cooking. Golf courses and tennis clubs host beginner classes. And job training is available for those who want to enter a new career.

So whatever you choose to do, as Nike says, "Just do it!"

The Lord is no respecter of age. When he looks for someone to serve him, he doesn't look at a birth certificate; he looks at the heart. Noah was four hundred eighty years old when the Lord commanded him to build an ark. Moses was eighty when the Lord appointed him to lead the Hebrews out of Egypt. Caleb was eighty-five when he drove giants from the mountain the Lord had promised to him. Rocking chairs would have been inappropriate retirement gifts for these men. You see, their lives were just beginning!

LORD, *may each new day radiate with magnificent opportunities and fresh challenges. Grant me the necessary faith, wisdom, and energy to make the most of them.*

Day 27: Past Your Prime?

He who began a good work in you will
perfect it until the day of Christ Jesus.
—Philippians 1:6 NASB

WHEN YOUNG Freddie Lindstrom came up as a rookie with the 1924 New York Giants, he had no idea that in six short months he would appear in a World Series. But there he was, playing third base in the twelfth inning of the seventh and deciding game. The rival Washington team had loaded the bases. Then a Washington batter hit a grounder. The speeding ball hit a pebble and bounced over Freddie's shoulder, enabling the winning run to score and costing the Giants the championship.

Although discouraged, Lindstrom rallied from this defeat and went on to become an outstanding player over the next decade. In 1935, however, Freddie was considered past his prime and over the hill. He became a throw-in in a six-player trade with Chicago.

Through the 1935 season the Cubs spent most of the year in third place, and Lindstrom spent most of his time on the bench. Then, on September 4, with only a month left in the season, Freddie got his chance. Inserted into the lineup because of an injury to a regular, he immediately began paying huge dividends. His timely hitting and fine fielding led the Cubs to an amazing twenty-one-game winning streak, catapulting them into first place. On September 27, the Cubs clinched the pennant behind Lindstrom's three hits and four runs batted in.

Freddie had convincingly demonstrated that he wasn't past his prime.

The Scriptures introduce us to a number of people who were either considered or thought themselves to be past their prime, only to realize that God had much left for them to do. One such example was Abraham.

In Genesis 15, God promised Abraham that his descendants would be as numerous as the stars in the sky (see v. 5). Although Abraham believed God, there was a problem. He was getting on in years, and to make matters worse, his wife, Sarah, was barren. After Sarah suggested that Abraham lie with her servant Hagar in hopes that she would bear him a child, he produced a son, Ishmael. At eighty-six Abraham had finally become a father. But God wasn't through with him yet.

Thirteen years later he appeared to Abraham again and promised that Abraham would be father to many nations. Sure enough, within a year Sarah miraculously conceived and Isaac was born. At one hundred years old Abraham and his ninety-year-old wife, Sarah, were certainly considered past their prime. But God's timing and faithfulness prevailed.

At times we all feel that our lives are useless and we have nothing to offer. However, the good news is that there is much we can still accomplish for the Lord. Seniors have so much to offer in the way of experience and availability. Instead of giving up and spending our days in a rocking chair, let's seek out opportunities for service in our churches and communities.

We're not past our prime until God calls us home. Until then there's plenty for us to do.

LORD, *help me to see my remaining years as opportunities to accomplish your purposes and fulfill your perfect plan.*

Day 28: Satch

Be faithful, even to the point of death,
and I will give you the crown of life.
—Revelation 2:10

HE WAS ONE of the greatest baseball players ever to play the game. For more than
twenty years he was considered the best
pitcher ever in the Negro Leagues. No team
wanted to face him. No batter wanted to
step in against him. He was devastating.

He was born Leroy Paige in Mobile,
Alabama, in 1906, the seventh of eleven children. As a youngster he worked as a porter's
helper carrying luggage at the local railway

depot and was tagged with the nickname that would stick all his life: Satchel.

By the time he reached his teens, Satch stood six foot three and, although he only weighed 130 pounds, he could really pitch. Each year, under the most difficult of situations, he would establish a raft of new pitching records. He, along with many other African-American stars, would ride all night in run-down buses and perform for meager pay (the pass-the-hat variety), waiting for the day when he might be allowed to play in the major leagues. Because he was paid by the game, Satch would often pitch every day in a different town.

In 1947, it happened. Branch Rickey signed the first black ballplayer, Jackie Robinson, to a contract with the Brooklyn team, signaling the beginning of the end of racial segregation in baseball. In 1948, at the advanced age of forty-two, Satch became the oldest rookie ever to play in the majors when he signed with the Cleveland Indians.

That year he won six games, lost only one, and helped the Indians win the American League pennant.

Satch pitched for another six years in the majors, entertaining fans and frustrating the opposition. When called on to pitch, Satch would shuffle slowly in from the bull pen and go into his special warm-up routine. He had a variety of pitches, none more notable than his "hesitation pitch," in which he would suddenly stop at the top of his windup, hesitate a couple of seconds, and then cut loose from a variety of angles. He baffled and angered so many hitters and umpires that the league finally banned the pitch, deeming it "too dangerous."

His many philosophical sayings have become as famous as his pitching. The following are his recommendations on how to stay young:

- Avoid fried meats, which anger up the blood.
- If your stomach disputes you, lie

down and pacify it with cool thoughts.
- Keep the juices flowing by jangling around gently as you move.
- Go very light on the vices, such as carrying on in society. The social ramble ain't restful.
- Avoid running at all times.
- Don't look back; something might be gaining on you.

Satch was a great example of perseverance. His faithful determination through the tough years finally paid huge dividends when he not only reached the majors, but was also eventually elected to baseball's Hall of Fame.

The Scriptures teach that one of the key virtues and proofs of our faith is perseverance. Being able to bear along cheerfully under various pressures and difficulties will bring peace with God and eternal reward in heaven. For Christians, the model of perseverance is Jesus himself. While on earth, he felt every trial and temptation we do, yet he never gave in. God promises never to give us more that we can handle, and we can be assured that every trial has its purpose, for our good and his glory.

LORD, *help me to see your gracious hand in everything that comes my way, and give me the grace to persevere.*

Day 29: Stuck in a Rut?

Because of the LORD's great love we are
not consumed, for his compassions never fail.
They are new every morning; great is your faithfulness.
—Lamentations 3:22–23

IT HAS BEEN said that change is the only constant. Nothing stays the same. Just think about how different life was in the early 1940s.

- World War II was raging.
- Everybody listened to *Amos 'n Andy*.
- Families gathered around the radio, not the television set.
- A good annual income was $5,200.

- An ice-cream cone cost a nickel.
- Few people locked their doors.
- Hardly any couples owned two cars.
- Streetcars rolled up and down city streets.
- The McDonald's fast-food chain was nonexistent.
- Moviegoers applauded newsreels showing the Allies winning the war effort.
- Iceboxes were common.
- Soda pop came in bottles.
- Coke was only a soft drink.
- Kids felt safe talking to strangers.
- Congregations sang hymns.
- Doctors made house calls.
- Microwaves were tiny ocean waves.
- Motorists honked when they passed other cars.
- Motorists rolled down the driver's window and gave hand signals.
- Popular music had a melody you could follow and words you could understand.

- Teachers paddled kids who misbehaved, and when their parents found out, they paddled the kids too.
- Operators placed telephone calls, and neighbors shared party lines.

We've come a long way since the early 1940s, haven't we? And many of the changes we have witnessed have been good. Thanks to changes in communication we can call family and friends on a cell phone or reach them by e-mail. Changes in transportation have made it possible to fly coast-to-coast in less than five hours. Engineering changes have made ground travel faster and more comfortable, appliances more user-friendly, and life more comfortable. And changes in the field of medicine have increased longevity.

But how willing are we to accept change? Are we open to new ideas if they are good ideas? Are we willing to try new ways to communicate? To take up a new hobby? To make new friends?

Although our Lord's character never changes—he is "the same yesterday and today and forever" (Heb. 13:8)—he brings change into our lives so we will grow. A post stuck in the ground doesn't grow and produce fruit, but a tree that keeps drinking in moisture, soaking up sunshine, and adjusting to the wind grows stronger and more productive with every passing year.

So let's not get stuck in a rut in our senior years. After all, the young people shouldn't have all the fun!

LORD, *help me to age gracefully, to open my mind to good ideas, and to open my life to new opportunities. Keep me from getting stuck in a rut. Protect me from tunnel vision, and expand my horizons. May faith and flexibility make me the kind of person you want me to be.*

Section 6 · DEATH

Day 30: Beat the Clock!

Do not boast about tomorrow,
for you do not know what a day may bring forth.
—Proverbs 27:1

ACCORDING TO the Death Clock, the predicted time of my death (Jim) is August 23, 2009. So I need to finish my contribution to this book by then.

The Death Clock is featured on the Web site, www.deathclock.com. If you visit this Web site, you can obtain your personal death date. All you have to do is answer a few simple questions. You will have to give your birth date and sex, then click on the normal death date, pessimistic death date, or optimistic death date. I clicked on normal.

I don't know how accurate the Death Clock is. Its calculations are simply educated guesses based on an average life span for your gender. But it certainly makes its Web site visitors ponder the future and treasure the present. After calculating your death date, the Web site tells you how many seconds remain in your life. You can watch the seconds wind down—or you can exit the Web site and do something productive with the precious time that flies so swiftly.

You remember the old TV show *Beat the Clock*, don't you? Contestants won prizes if they completed a task (usually a weird task) in an allotted time. So they raced to beat the clock. Unlike that sometimes-wacky game show, beating the Death Clock means outlasting the deadline. And I'm sure that's precisely what you and I hope to do. But if we depart for heaven sooner than later, we can go with the victorious attitude that "to live is Christ and to die is gain" (Phil. 1:21).

Now, here's terrific news. The man or woman who honors the Lord is immortal until his or her life's work is done. I don't think the Death Clock takes that fact into consideration. I expect to live until the day I have completed the tasks the Lord gives me to do. My walk with the Lord down here will end, only to resume up there. I'm not concerned about the time my number will be up, because I know the One who puts the numbers up. In the meantime, I will value quality of time far more than quantity of years.

How about you?

LORD, *help me to number my days and incline my heart unto wisdom, to commit today to you and leave the future in your hands.*

Day 31: Eva

Well done, good and faithful servant! …
Come and share your master's happiness!
—Matthew 25:21

WHEN EVA RETIRED from her job, she had no idea what she would do with the rest of her life. Her husband had died many years before, and she was now somewhat free to do what she pleased in newfound retirement.

One of Eva's sisters had moved to Florida to care for their elderly mother and wanted her to move down and help. Eva decided to go. She found a small place in the same neighborhood and began a decade of loving care, which would last until her mother's death.

Eva attended church services regularly, but was obviously limited in her involvement. After her mother died, she began to look for ways to help.

She had never learned to drive, and although totally dependent on public transportation, she would not let that stop her from serving in the church. Timing bus routes and transfer points meticulously, she was able to get to church in about forty minutes. Eva began volunteering for just about any need the church had. She packed boxes of food and clothes for the poor, made pies and cakes for dinners and banquets, and greeted visitors with her winning smile.

One day, Eva noticed a plea in the church bulletin for a preschool leader in the Sunday school. Week after week, she tried to ignore the tugging that was going on inside of her. She resisted because of her age and transportation difficulties. Finally, after a month of struggle, Eva took the position, thus beginning one of the most joyous and fulfilling times of her life. Each week would find her getting to church an hour before class time. She would enthusiastically get the classroom ready with visuals and projects for the early comers. Then she would cheerfully greet each of the children as they arrived. At eighty, Eva had found the one thing in life that satisfied her the most—pouring herself into the lives of little children.

One night, while working at home on crafts for her class, she decided she needed something from the store. On the way back, she was struck by a car. She regained consciousness only long enough to give the nurse the name and phone number of her only son, then died early the next morning.

At Eva's funeral, the pastor made note of her favorite verse, "For to me, to live is Christ and to die is gain" (Phil. 1:21). Indeed, her life was lived to the glory of God, as she faithfully served her family and her children.

Some have wondered why God would allow such a violent death for such a loving servant. Maybe it was an answer to a request Eva herself made. After caring for her mother, she would say, "I hope the Lord takes me quickly, so I don't have to be a burden on anyone." It may not have been the way she envisioned, but the Lord certainly answered her prayer.

LORD, *thank you for the life of this faithful servant, and help us to remember that we are never too old to respond when you call us to serve you.*

Day 32: No Fear of Dying

So do not fear, for I am with you; do not be dismayed,
for I am your God. I will strengthen you and help you;
I will uphold you with my righteous right hand.
—Isaiah 41:10

BUS, TRAIN, and automobile are forms of travel preferred by thousands of Americans who are afraid to fly. Football commentator John Madden refused to fly. So he crisscrossed the country by bus to do each *Monday Night Football* show. Thousands more are afraid of heights, so they stay off rooftops and mountain peaks. Others, who are afraid of the number thirteen, would never sign a rental agreement for a thirteenth-floor apartment.

Of course, we can't always avoid situations that cause us to fear. Then, too, most people are afraid to die, but sooner or later they will experience death. Christians, however, can look beyond death to a wonderful life in heaven with Jesus.

Although the following story's source is unknown, it presents a comforting reason not to fear death.

Before leaving the examination room, a sick man confided in his Christian doctor, who practiced medicine in a private area of his home. "Doctor, I am afraid to die. Tell me what lies on the other side."

Quietly, the doctor replied, "I don't know."

Suddenly the two men heard scratching and whining on the other side of a door leading into the examination room. When the doctor opened the door, his dog sprang into the room and leaped on him with obvious delight.

Turning to the patient, the doctor explained, "My dog has never been in this room. He didn't know what was inside. But he knew his master was here, and when I opened the door, he sprang in without fear. I know little of what is on the other side of death, but I do know one thing—my Master is there, and that is good enough for me."

The Bible actually tells us more about hell than heaven, but what it does tell us about heaven leads us to conclude that it is a beautiful, delightful place. But the best reason to anticipate heaven is the fact that Jesus is there. After passing through death's door, we will see him face-to-face (see 1 John 3:2).

LORD, *thank you for conquering death and removing the fear of leaving this life behind. Thank you, too, for opening heaven's door for all who believe.*

Day 33: On the Lone Prairie

Now we know that if the earthly tent we live
in is destroyed, we have a building from God,
an eternal house in heaven, not built by human hands.
—2 Corinthians 5:1

WHOEVER WROTE "Bury me not on the lone prairie" must not have cherished the thought of tumbleweeds blowing over his grave. Or did he want to spare surviving relatives and friends visiting his grave a long trip from town? Have you wondered where he preferred to be buried?

While some Christians are opting for cremation, others oppose it on the grounds that believers in biblical times were buried. Of course, if these Christians insisted on following the biblical precedent to the letter, wouldn't they insist on being buried in a tomb? The facts are, death destroys the body, the tent in which the deceased spent his or her life, and after death the body turns to dust. So, does it really matter where a believer's body gets buried or his ashes get stored or scattered?

When Jesus returns in the air and shouts, "Come forth," the buried body will rise. The earth will roll aside like a discarded blanket, and the human remains will quickly become a glorified and incorruptible body. As for cremated remains—ashes—they, too, will become a glorified, incorruptible body. The God who formed Adam from the dust of the earth can certainly form a resurrected body from dust!

What a climactic, dramatic, and dynamic event the resurrection of the dead will be. The Christian dead will rise from all parts of the planet. Even the lone prairie will be included. In the final analysis, our so-called final resting place has no eternal significance. What matters for eternity is the blessedness of resting our faith in Jesus.

LORD, *I will rejoice today in the assurance that to be absent from the body is to be present with you.*

Day 34: Our Final Reunion

We will be with the Lord forever.
—1 Thessalonians 4:17

THE OLDER WE get, the more reunions we're invited to—and each time, there seems to be fewer and fewer present. A friend recently quipped, "Pretty soon we'll be having these in a closet."

Some folks view reunions with mixed emotions. Although it's nice to see and visit with old friends and family, these times can also become occasions for reopening old wounds. All in all, though, most reunions are happy opportunities to revisit with acquaintances and relive past memories.

My (Joe's) mother loved going to her annual high school reunion. Each year she would faithfully migrate back to Decatur, Illinois, where she was raised, to reconnect with fellow students, friends, and even some teachers. She would always recount how some had changed in appearance. "Donald has lost just about all his hair, and Margaret has certainly put on a lot of weight." Or she would comment on their changed lives, "Herb just retired, and his son is running his company now." Then, there would always be a sad time of reflection when the names of those who had died during the past year were read. As each person stood in quiet respect, many wondered at what future reunion their name would be read. For Mom it was 1993.

And how about those family reunions? We had one a few years ago that attracted people from all over the country. I remember the phone ringing constantly with lost relatives asking for directions. When we all finally got together, it was fun seeing how the little cousins, nephews, and nieces had grown into adults. Many had brought their children, which prompted us to try to figure out the proper relational descriptions. I think there was a second nephew's cousin running around. The dinner was something to behold—pounds of meat grilled to perfection, along with pies and cakes prepared especially for the occasion.

Suddenly, at the height of activity, the lights blinked momentarily and then went out altogether. There was just enough daylight left to gather everybody outside for the obligatory family picture.

After everyone left, my wife and I sat by flickering candles and recounted a wonderful day.

Someday, believers in Christ will experience the ultimate reunion. The Bible teaches that when that happens we will see Jesus face-to-face, and we will actually be like him, for we will see him as he is. Our reunion in heaven will be marked by a number of extraordinary benefits. No sin, no sickness, no pain, no tears, and no darkness are but a few. But the best is that we will be with the Lord.

LORD, *when situations discourage us in this life, help us to remember we belong to you and to eagerly anticipate our reunion with you in heaven.*

Day 35: Partnership Dissolved

He who finds a wife finds what is good
and receives favor from the LORD.
—Proverbs 18:22

RAY AND BETTIE were as close as a married couple could be. They shared life's good times and rough times. They raised three fine sons. In their younger years, they taught two- and three-year-olds in Sunday school. They faithfully attended church throughout their married years. They supported their church and missionaries financially. They worked hard, probably harder than most couples, but they never complained, not even when painful adversity struck them.

Ray underwent several surgeries, and Bettie developed arthritis in her hands. When they were about fifty, they lost their middle son when his gun accidentally discharged and a bullet penetrated his head.

Later, Ray left his job as an art director and production manager. He and Bettie sold their house, moved into a rental unit, bought typesetting equipment, and started a typesetting and design business. Ray pounded the pavement in search of clients and designed brochures and newsletters. Bettie set type and proofread. Both worked long hours. When their business grew, they hired one of their sons as a helper.

Finally, the two retired; that is, as retired as they could let themselves be. They still set type and designed material for their son, the business's new owner. Ray also worked as a part-time jobber for printers.

They were nearing eighty when Bettie

learned she had liver cancer and only a short time left to live. As an act of deep love for Ray, she wrote a manual of instructions for him on how to run the household appliances and prepare his favorite meals. A less devoted wife of modern bent might simply give her husband directions to the nearest McDonald's. But Bettie was from the old school, and she was not about to go to heaven without first taking care of her husband of fifty-six years.

Bettie's memorial service was one of triumph, and Ray took comfort in knowing he would see her again in a far better place. He may never win every bout with loneliness, but he thanks the Lord for his faithful presence and for a wife with whom he shared an enduring love.

In Ephesians 5:22–33, the apostle Paul alluded to the self-sacrificing love Christ showered on his bride, the church, by dying for her. A Christian marriage lasts and thrives when the husband and wife cherish each other as Christ cherishes the church. Death may interrupt the flow of their love for each other, but it cannot destroy it.

If your spouse is still by your side, give him or her a hug and say "I love you." If your spouse is deceased, cherish his or her memory and the love you shared. Someday you will be together again.

LORD, *I thank you for your sacrificial love. I feel so undeserving but grateful. May I be an instrument of your love today, whether I am at home or away from home.*

Section 7 · PLANNED LIVING

Day 36: All Nursing Centers Are Not Created Equal

Surely goodness and love will follow me all the days of my life,
and I will dwell in the house of the LORD forever.
—Psalm 23:6

PASTOR GENE knows all nursing centers are not created equal. When he visits Millie at Shady Grove, he can't help noticing a foul odor. It permeates the halls. Also, Millie tells him her meals are often cold and unappetizing. However, when he visits William at Oak Creek Manor, he is impressed with its immaculate conditions, pleasant caregivers, and well-groomed residents. According to

William, the food tastes great, and he gets to choose a special dessert at dinner.

Wouldn't life be grand if every senior could live independently at home for the next forty years? Unfortunately, failing health or the unavailability of an at-home caregiver mandates that a parent or spouse move into a nursing center. If the choice of a nursing center falls to you, how will you choose the right one? Here are a few suggestions:

Consider the cost. Do you have adequate long-term health care insurance? Does the nursing center accept Medicare or Medicaid? What does the daily rate deliver to a resident? Are additional fees slapped on for certain services?

Check out the facilities. Are the rooms and furnishings adequate or cramped and sparse? Is the center clean and inviting? Is it quiet, or must the residents endure traffic noises? Is it free of offensive odors? Does it provide a pleasant dining area, a solarium or outdoor patio, and an exercise area?

Ask about the food. Get the opinions of several residents about the food. Is it well prepared, tasty, varied, served promptly, and in generous portions? Are snacks available?

Observe the staff. Is there an adequate number of nurses and assistants? Stroll down a hall, peer into residents' rooms, and observe how many nurse call lights are on. Is the staff friendly and neatly attired?

Ask to see a schedule of activities. Does the nursing center provide a full program of activities, or is there very little for the residents to do? Can the residents gather comfortably to watch TV or play table games? Are chapel services conducted regularly?

Because you want to choose the best nursing center at the most reasonable cost, you need to do some comparison shopping.

An Old Testament king's grandson needed constant care from the time he was five. That's when an accident left him lame in both feet. But neither his father, Jonathan, nor his grandfather, King Saul, could take care of him, because they were killed in battle. However, years later when David became king, he found Mephibosheth and brought him to the royal residence. There, he treated Mephibosheth as one of his own sons, set a place for him at the king's table, and gave him farmland and a corps of servants to work the land (see 2 Sam. 9:1–13).

What King David did for Mephibosheth prefigured what Jesus does for each of his followers. Even the most comfortable nursing center cannot rival such care. We can say joyfully, "He has taken me to the banquet hall, and his banner over me is love" (Song 2:4).

LORD, *I do not deserve your care, but I thank you for it. It is profound and perfect. May I rest in your protection and delight in your provision today, tomorrow, and always.*

Day 37: Every Neighborhood Needs a "Granny"

Be kind and compassionate to one another.
—Ephesians 4:32

ALTHOUGH SHE has never been a grandmother, everyone knows her as "Granny." Maybe that's because she displays the love and kindness of the best grandmas.

Granny never married. She retired long ago from her job in the county clerk's office, a position she held for thirty-one years. She has lived in the same house and in the same neighborhood for more than forty years. Now, in her mid-eighties, she is more than content to live out her life where she has always lived—among her friends and family.

Although retired, Granny is far from inactive. She keeps track of everyone's birthday or anniversary so she can send a special card or greeting. Plus, she never fails to send an encouraging note to those who are sick or hospitalized. She has watched dozens of neighborhood children grow up and have kids of their own, and she rarely forgets a name. All the kids know her too. Many make Granny's house a regular stop on the way home from school or while playing. There, they are sure to find fresh home-baked cookies or yummy treats. And more than a few times, her sensible, down-home advice has soothed and mended a broken heart.

When someone suggested that she might consider moving to the retirement center recently completed in her area, Granny refused to consider the advice. "I have everything I need right here," she said. "And I would really miss all my friends."

Knowing how to handle the retirement years can be harder than anticipated for seniors. Many have to deal with health issues and are forced to relocate to other areas. Others have financial pressures that cause them to leave their familiar surroundings to find more affordable housing. Some refuse to consider retirement, choosing to work indefinitely. Tough choices for sure!

But for Granny the choice was simple. She would just keep doing what she had always done. She would keep on reflecting the love and kindness of the source of love and kindness. Granny personally knows the love of the Lord Jesus and enjoys demonstrating that love to whomever he places in her path or on her porch.

LORD, *give me a desire to show the love and kindness you so generously show me.*

Day 38: Exercising Your Faith

But grow in the grace and knowledge
of our Lord and Savior Jesus Christ.
—2 Peter 3:18

WHY DON'T more seniors exercise?

This question points out a critical need in the older adult community. Why don't the elderly exercise on a regular basis? Some experts believe many seniors are afraid of hurting themselves or of suffering a heart attack or stroke if they exert themselves. Actually, the opposite is true. Moderate exercise can strengthen the cardiovascular system, improve circulation, build endurance and stamina, and, for those with diabetes, reduce harmful blood sugar. And the exercise doesn't have to involve hours of sweaty weight lifting and stair climbing. Just a twenty-to-thirty-minute brisk walk three or four times a week is enough to keep a senior in shape both physically and mentally.

However, many seniors have been conditioned (the wrong way) by a society that thinks the older we get the more we need to rest and just take life easy. Many of our elderly prematurely find their way into nursing homes where they sit around all day watching TV and then go to bed.

Yet, according to the experts, no group in our society can benefit more from exercise than senior citizens. The muscles of the elderly are just as responsive as those of younger people. And a study at Boston's Brigham and Women's Hospital shows women can reduce their risk of breast cancer through regular exercise. Women who walked three to five hours per week had a

50 percent lower risk of dying from the malignancy!

Using the same principle and applying it spiritually, we can all benefit greatly as we exercise our faith. The Bible clearly teaches that we are to continually grow in the Lord. Studying God's Word and spending time in prayer is the best antidote to developing a flabby faith that buckles easily under the trials and pressures of life. Renewing our minds as we revitalize our bodies gives us a tremendous advantage as we face the problems aging can bring.

So do yourself a favor and take a walk, and be sure it's with the King.

LORD, *help us to see that our bodies and our minds are a great gift from you. Give us the grace and strength to exercise both for your glory.*

Day 39: How Firm a Foundation!

Therefore everyone who hears these words of mine
and puts them into practice is like a wise man who built
his house on the rock. The rain came down, the streams rose,
and the winds blew and beat against that house; yet it did
not fall, because it had its foundation on the rock.
—Matthew 7:24–25

BIRD-WATCHERS in Florida can easily spot a "snowbird." The state has thousands of them. They have migrated from the North— Canada, Iowa, Minnesota, Wisconsin, Illinois, Michigan, Ohio, and New York—and nested in warm, sunny Florida. Most "snowbirds" are retirees; some plopped down most of their life savings on a house near a beach, either on the Gulf Coast or on the Atlantic side. Others opted for a less expensive mobile home. However, you can find the "snowbird" nests inland as well as along the coasts; that is, you could, before the horrendous hurricanes of 2004 destroyed so many of them. Hurricanes Charley, Frances, and Ivan chased thousands of residents from their homes, knocked out power, blew houses off their foundations, and flooded communities. Many seniors returned to find nothing standing on their property.

But Florida was not the only state to experience hurricane damage. Ivan rushed through Gulf Coast states and stampeded as far north as New Jersey, leaving ruined houses and gaping, scarred landscapes in its path. It also left a message: Houses are defenseless against nature's fury. If we think walls, a floor, and a roof protect us in all kinds of situations, we need to think again. Remember the horrendous devastation Katrina caused in Louisiana, Mississippi, and Alabama in 2005!

Nevertheless, Christians have a secure home in heaven. Jesus is the Builder, and what he, the Carpenter of Nazareth, puts together is far superior to even a billionaire's earthly mansion. It is built to last forever. Furthermore, we won't have to make a single mortgage payment. There are no property taxes or association dues. We won't have to pay homeowners insurance to be "in good hands," because we will be in Jesus' hands. Hurricanes may buffet us down here, but peaceful conditions prevail up there. Even the most discriminating "snowbirds" will admit that the comfort and beauty of heaven exceeds even that of Florida at its best.

LORD, *help those who have experienced natural disaster to recover, and help me to keep my heart fixed on the eternal.*

Day 40: The Little Engine That Could

Therefore, I urge you, brothers, in view of God's mercy,
to offer your bodies as living sacrifices, holy and pleasing
to God—this is your spiritual act of worship.
—Romans 12:1

DURING WORLD WAR II, our country was called upon to make many difficult sacrifices that contributed to the war effort. Every news item, it seemed, related to some shortage or need brought about by the fighting taking place overseas.

As a four-year-old, I (Joe) watched neighbors plant "Victory Gardens" to grow vegetables and fruit. Sewing circles, as they were called, made blankets and sheets that were sent to Red Cross units to help as they treated casualties.

Just about every street corner in our neighborhood had a large metal container chained to a light pole for the collection of discarded or donated items made of steel. These items would be used to make guns, bullets, tanks, and even planes. Each day at play, I would see those barrels and wonder what I could contribute. I didn't have very many steel toys, except the wind-up train I had received for Christmas a few months before.

One day, I asked my mother if it was okay to donate the engine, since it was the heaviest, and would obviously be more valuable. Although she was touched that I would donate such a prized possession, she suggested I give one of the other cars so I would still have a usable train. I insisted that the other cars were only made of tin, and whoever heard of tin bullets? She relented, and the next day I proudly dropped my beloved engine into the corner scrap barrel.

Sometimes seniors can get the mistaken impression they have nothing to contribute. Some feel their financial limitations or health problems restrict them from doing anything significant for others. Yet there are many opportunities for older individuals to be involved in vital situations where their help is desperately needed. Local hospitals, libraries, schools, senior centers, and churches are just a few of the possibilities for senior service.

So look around for a scrap barrel that needs your special engine. You'll be glad you did.

LORD, *help me to be sensitive to the needs of those around me. Give me the desire and grace to help meet those needs. Amen.*

About the Authors

JOE RAGONT *has been involved in the Christian community for nearly forty years. He owns and manages Ragont Design, a graphic design firm serving primarily Christian publishers and organizations. His company provides creative design and copy writing for books, catalogs, newsletters, brochures, etc. He has written and illustrated dozens of Bible-based leaders' guides and overhead transparency programs. For over twenty-five years he has led a weekly Bible study for men, and he is constantly sought after for teaching and speaking opportunities.*

Joe and his wife, Pat, live in Inverness, Illinois, and are members of the Arlington Heights Evangelical Free Church. They have four grown children and two grandchildren.

Born in Scotland, JIM DYET *emigrated to Canada with his parents in 1939. After completing high school in St. Catharines, Ontario, he attended Moody Bible Institute in Chicago, where he graduated as class president. Jim also holds a BA degree in religion from Houghton College, Houghton, New York, and the following degrees from Louisiana Baptist University, Shreveport,*

Louisiana: MA in theology, ThD in English Bible, and an honorary DLit. He has also pursued graduate studies in counseling at Indiana State University and pastoral theology at the Denver Seminary respectively.

Jim has authored more than forty Bible curriculum courses, hundreds of articles, and sixteen books. From 1971 until 2000, Jim held positions of executive editor and managing editor for Accent Publications, youth and adult editor for Regular Baptist Press, and managing editor for Scripture Press. During his curriculum editorial career, he traveled extensively as a conference speaker for Christian education conferences.

Currently Jim serves as senior pastor at Calvary Bible Church, Colorado Springs, and is a member of the Jerry B. Jenkins Christian Writers Guild's editorial board. He also mentors 180 Guild students. He and his wife, Gloria, have been married forty-seven years and reside in Colorado Springs. Their two adult daughters, an adult son, and two granddaughters reside in Denver.